Thank you for using my book!
I hope you enjoyed it.
Please leave a rating on Amazon.

Visit my website at wingsablazeart.com